Torch the Empty Fields

New Women's Voices Series, No. 171

poems by

Mary Jo LoBello Jerome

Finishing Line Press
Georgetown, Kentucky

Torch the Empty Fields

Copyright © 2022 by Mary Jo LoBello Jerome
ISBN 979-8-88838-051-2 First Edition
All rights reserved under International and Pan-American Copyright Conventions. No part of this book may be reproduced in any manner whatsoever without written permission from the publisher, except in the case of brief quotations embodied in critical articles and reviews.

ACKNOWLEDGMENTS

In appreciation to the editors who first published these poems, sometimes in different forms, in their journals and anthologies:

> *A Certain Kind of Swagger* : "Tulips in Midwinter"
> *Fire Up the Poems* : "Lightning Strikes"
> *Literary North* : "Tomato Intuition"
> *Ovunque Siamo* : "Gracie Clara Angie Rose," "We Lived Where, How," "Dressing Yourself," and "Broken Monster Sonnets"
> *Paterson Literary Review* : "I Dream What My Mother Means to Say"
> *Philadelphia Stories* : "The Masterpiece in Our Bedroom"
> *Poets Reading the News* : "Torch the Empty Fields"
> *River Heron Review* : "Tokyo Underground Prayer"
> *Schuylkill Valley Journal* : "Lemon Tree Haiku," "How to Eat Raw Herring" and "A Black Stone"
> *Stillwater Review* : "Twenty"
> *US 1 Worksheets* : "Vreeland Avenue"

Publisher: Leah Huete de Maines
Editor: Christen Kincaid
Cover Art and Design: Ariele Rosch
Author Photo: Laura Pedrick Photography

Order online: www.finishinglinepress.com
also available on amazon.com

Author inquiries and mail orders:
Finishing Line Press
P. O. Box 1626
Georgetown, Kentucky 40324
U. S. A.

Table of Contents

I

Kissing Windows on a Pandemic Summer Day 1
Torch the Empty Fields 2
Inflammatory Response 4
The Season of Ash 5
What Distance Means 6
The Wheels on the Bus 7
Ghost Dogs 8
Photo Stream Denial 9
Peacock Time 10
Three Women 11
Now, Even Birds Are to Blame 13

II

Lightning Strikes 17
Broken Monster Sonnets 18
The Auction 19
I Dream What My Mother Means to Say 20
Flooded Odette's 22
Twenty 23
A Rural Metal Mailbox 24
Vreeland Avenue 25
How to Eat Raw Herring 26
Gracie Clara Angie Rose 27
My Missile Crisis, 1962 29
Winter Dinner 30
Mark Has a Thing or Two to Say About Those
    Strollers & Moms 32

III

Tomato Intuition 35

We Lived Where, How 36

Dressing Yourself 38

Tulips in Midwinter 39

Seeds 40

The Human Sundial at Jacob's Well 41

Still, I Smudged the House with Sage 42

Lemon Tree Haiku 44

A Black Stone 45

Tokyo Underground Prayer 46

Hotaru Ika : Firefly Squid 48

The Masterpiece in Our Bedroom 49

My Daughter's Snakes 50

for Ariele and Sara

*Have you ever noticed how the trees
change from state to state?*

Ada Limón, "Of Roots and Roamers"

I

Then, too, it often pays to torch sterile fields,
and to scorch with crackling flame the wisps of stubble,
whether soil draws strength unseen and rich sustenance
from fire, or that by flame corruption's pasteurized away.

Virgil's Georgics, A Poem of the Land
1: 84-88, translated by Kimberly Johnson

Kissing Windows on a Pandemic Summer Day

He flattens his lips on the plate window of the store front. Inside,
the mannequins wear face masks. He kisses the glass in a line

like nibbling an ear of corn. Greasy lip prints smudge through
grime and soot. I'm at the corner in a crowd, aware of heat

and distance, waiting for the light. We watch but avoid his eyes.
Sir? Sir? a girl calls. *Don't do that. It's a fact. You'll fetch germs.*

Fetch. Not catch. She's not from here.
Someone needs to take him home.

94 degrees. No answer but sweat and shrugs. He rails to the still-life
models dressed in lime and pink spring outfits—a mini dress,

a pants suit, tan handbags, medical face coverings—
Don't don't don't. Where is it? Julia! Pick up the phone.

What he says exactly, I don't know. But how he says it, jesus.
When he leans his forehead on his reflection, tete-a-tete, I imagine

he whispers street corner secrets in the sun to the Julia he can't visit.
What he needs—these mannequins overdressed for a day on the town

can't give him. When the pedestrian signal lights up, the mom from
elsewhere pulls her girl to the crosswalk, *Someone will fetch the police.*

Later at home with the neat row of salvia and vinca out front in the shade,
I tell this story and regret I made it funny. So I tell it again. The right way.

Torch the Empty Fields

My friend, the writer, applied for a permit
from the town for a bonfire to burn
the wreckage of this year in effigy.
She'd use the broken limbs from dead trees,
cracked shutters that hid a pulsing colony
of angry wasps, the rotted rescue ladder
dangling over the steep riverbank.
That's what she told the town.

On the invite she wrote: *Let the flames burn
the stubble away. Bring kindling—Amazon
cartons, election junk mail, the neighbor's
lawn signs, splinters of anger, your bruises.
Let's make ashy feathers for our hopes.
Wear your masks.*

I called to see if this was a real thing
or a poem. She said, both.
Sometimes her work is a wink and a nod.
Sometimes it's urgent. I brought a thermos
of hot bourbon toddies to help me through.

The first thing she burned was the denial
from the officials in the closed town hall.
Whole tree trunks formed a pyramid pyre
over shorter logs, planks, and abandoned
junk from a collapsing shed. The arms and legs
of seatless chairs, a shattered chest missing
drawers, skeletal picture frames, vague pieces
of wood that once were something else—
all flared and disintegrated in flame.

In October's thin air, sparks leapt amber
and wild. Dots of stars peeked through holes
in smoke thermals like embers. We dropped
our blankets and coats in disheveled heaps,
piles of bodies in the long shadows.

The blaze pushed us back and back, widening
our circle until no one could speak. The heat
and energy explosive enough I thought someone
might strip naked and howl. Or combust.
That's how ready we were.

Inflammatory Response

Singapore, then Austin in one week.
Breathing, oh breathing, was hard. No escaping

the muggy, tropical lush of dense fronds,
the damp undernotes of spores and earth decay.

The tangled jungle was close, though the hard-baked
streets were wide and clean. At the thronged, hot

wet-market, I wheezed in the mist of puddles volatilized
from melted ice and fish blood. Then, a stop in Texas

with its dry spring on the verge of drought. Cedar pollen
dusted green the handrails, car hoods, windowpanes.

Every arid surface, finely powdered and scorching.
The scrabbly woods around the kids' house, thirsty

and bleached pale. Back home, asthma aflame from
the offending flora and feathery air, all those invisible,

inhalable motes carried on deceptive breezes—treacherous
birch, white pine, oak, and ash—a futile conflict. I'm armed

only with meager weaponry: daily pills, sprays, inhalers, gaspy
prayers. Palliative illusions, no cures, no true compromise.

I try not to read the aggravating news. I learn that pollen
grains are male. This body at war, swollen mucousy trachea,

its subconscious battle of cells, a country divisible, killing
itself bit by bit in habitual squabbles. There are days, panting,

that I wish for something big and biblical to cleanse
the world, to trade everything for clarity, a flood

of clear air, a shining do-over so we
can breathe easy again, trust our one body.

The Season of Ash

"I'll have no truck with the devil's creations now."
G. Turner

The smoke is rising. This is what I'll

keep from the notes I have

scribbled these last flaming days. No

spring tender shoots, no mountain of mulch the truck

dumped in the yard, nothing of the pots heavy with

iris, catmint, bee balm planted where the devil's

hair took over the wet, woody corner. Creations

in the garden fade like ash in the hurt of now.

What Distance Means

"We are only as sick as our secrets and our shame."

We don't—we can't—touch. We don't talk. Long miles are not all we
have put between us. Craggy cliffs, deserts, unwadable rivers. Are

you well? The outbreak's origin, the burning buildings, only
minutes from your house—I know from the news. Smoke, virus, gunfire as

close as breath. I used to think it was solely me who was sick
and broken, but not in this country, this spring. All this loss wretched as

unnamed, unearthed bones. Isolation, outrage, smothered truth, not our
story alone as if our wounds were harbingers. These secrets

borne like baskets of stones. Buried truths and our
unattended pain, not just ours, but time's grave, shared shame.

The Wheels on the Bus

On Sixth Street heading to eat with the kids
and the baby who's just learning to say
mine and goes *vroom* for all the moving cars
and busses dashing through his limited
line of vision, we stop at the light near
the shelter. A barefoot woman, naked
save for a man's sleeveless teeshirt tightly
pulled over her buttocks, tiptoe-runs
as if in heels on the cold sidewalk, white legs,
tangled hair, loose breasts bouncing and roughly
visible through thin, cotton fabric.
Where I grew up, they called those undershirts
guinea tees. For us guineas. Today, we all
wear them: beaters. Right? No joke.

Who's kidding? Language changes, and we stay
the same. The wheels on the world go
round and round, beep beep goes a horn.
Two blue police chatting at the crosswalk—
the tee-shirted woman scurries behind,
stretches the hem to her thighs, crosses
her arm on her chest to cover cleavage,
tries for smallness. Did I plead out loud
at the window to the cops: *turn around,
look now, turn around,* because the baby
mimics and sings. The cops pivot, and when
I think our wish lands safe, they simply watch
her trot up the cool street of cafes. Beep
beep, the light changes, vroom vroom goes our car.

Ghost Dogs

No such thing as distance,
shadow catcher.

An hour before daylight,
local visitations : evidence of things unseen,
ghost dogs,
all god's dangers.

Everything counts.
dread islands : a suitcase of seaweed,
horoscopes for the dead.

A car stops and a door opens : the crossing.

Next,
nice people,
all the pretty horses,
the minor virtues.

Photo Stream Denial

A double rainbow floated fairy soft
over farmland and shimmered long enough
for me to take a picture, capture it,
call to strangers on the road—*See that?*
I cropped that photo, posted it, and bragged
I'd make a mint printing a greeting card.

And now? In this sharp hardened place, I see
in the sky only fierce white rims around
darkening clouds. They fight their fight alone.
Sleep eludes them. Morning arrives like sludge.
Collisions would be the only spark in the day.
If the sun could eat us, they'd say yes.

Peacock Time

1.
My friend near the river marks the days since three
peafowl came to roost in her tree. Now one is dead
and two rescued to a farm. *Or stolen away*, she bitterly says.
Colorless, quiet, less pungent days. All the negative space.

2.
The neighbor kids caw. It's a zoo. One kid tosses
a crumbled Kashi bar. One runs in circles, flapping. The birds
flutter and hop, too keen on morsels to fly away. My friend,
shrill: *Stay away from the water. Jesus, where are your parents?*

Two girls, messy braids, dusty elbows, heedless of peacocks
or adults, measure each other and crow. *In dance, we go round
and round.* They stamp their feet when they twirl: *Now. One, two.
Now.* Again. And again. Whirling, squealing, dizzy in the grass.

The peacocks quaver. The eyes of their fanned feathers
flit like monster bugs. The quills vibrate. One bird bobs,
wary, then stretches and struts. The dowdy peahen pecks a tin pan
of mealworms and fruit. Girls dance under the roosting tree.

This day is caught edgewise between the seconds before, the hours
not yet. A mom appears and sets a timer on her phone. *In five
minutes, we're leaving.* When it chirps down, she yells, *Say
thank you to Miss Cathie.* Kids grab water bottles. No one argues.

The birds scream like the jungle surrounds them
in Lambertville, New Jersey. The girls cover their ears,
count the calls. The spindled crest of the largest bird
pulsates with each cry and shriek. Three, at first. A rest. Then two.

3.
The short period of the peacocks was joy, was brilliant, was …
My friend doesn't know how to say it. Bare-kneed in the grit,
she shooed cats, tolerated children, offered seeds in naked palms,
begged the bulbous, iridescent birds for a little more time.

Three Women

at a table, coffee mugs, danish picked to crumbs
       reading glasses, cheerios, cheese,
             a notebook, ice in a glass, a bird guide
one remembered makeup   one forgot the peanut allergies
       one asked for wet wipes
                          one failed to sing
           one folded the laundry   one neglected her name
     one recited everyone's name plus her own
                        one ignored the day
          one picked up all the kids
       one heard a joke, a pussy & a snort
         one denied she shaved her legs
one shut the phone   one put the kids out of the car a mile before home
    one thought to ask about drugs
        one did not check the doorknob
          one locked the windows
     one climbed down and ran   one caught   one threw
one didn't see the broken glass   one hit the snarling dog
        one saved   one told her friends
           one bet the house   one prayed for silence
     one walked through hallways listening   one turned over rocks
one fell to her knees   one licked the sandwich edges
          one built caves with coats and chairs
    one confused loss and the lost
          one was an octopus   one sat on a box and averted her eyes

                         one carried a clown bag of tricks
one worked all night in a trance   one remained married
               one didn't call her mother   one polished her mother's nails
one slammed   one shhhhsssed
                         one wouldn't talk to all the kids
one had grandchildren   one moved, house to trailer to room
      one sought the aurora   one quit and quit again
one dug through the dirt   one slapped the hand away
     one didn't let her head jerk back   one refused the news
                one flipped the pages   one held on and on
one looked and lifted   one keeled   one kept it all

Now, Even Birds Are to Blame

after W. Steginsky

The grackles are back, packs of them, looming
over the feeders we filled and watched so
religiously this isolation year.
The cold weather regulars are gone—juncos,
cardinals—even the dove couple who
cooed us through our covid mourning doesn't
offer their soulful songs on the deck rails,
the gang of greedy grackles at their tails.
We thought the unsettling was ending
but we're smack stuck in the midst of it all.
Yesterday under the window, I found
the pulsing tiny body of a ruby
-throated hummingbird, small enough to nest
in a lichen-lined tablespoon. I covered
it with a terry towel up to the eye,
its needle beak exposed to the air,
and watched the cloth rapidly rise and fall,
rise and fall,
                until it woke and wanted out.
When I raised the cloth, it flashed into
flight, buzzing at face height before it flew
off. Sizing me up as someone to thank
or one of those blue-headed creatures who
chased it to the glass? The grackles. I hate them.
A lifetime ago I might have lifted palms up
to accept this world in any of its shapes.
To do as my friend did one empty, cold night,
startled around a shadowed bend of road
by the vision of a fat luminous moon—
she said simply—*Let this be enough.*
But now, the grackle rusty-hinge chatter
scrapes through the yard. It's too much
after everything else. The moon's not enough.
Not hummingbirds. Not prayer. It's time for fire.

II

So by decree
all things incline to worse, and foundering backslide,
back like one whose oar can scarcely thrust his skiff upstream;
if perchance he slack his arms, sternward
the coursing water drags him down the rapids.

Virgil's Georgics, A Poem of the Land
1:199-204, translated by Kimberly Johnson

Lightning Strikes

"How do you teach your child to breathe when the world takes your air?"
after Deborah D.E.E.P. Mouton

We watch the roiling storm from the riverbank. How
close will it get before we run or react? I don't know. Do
you? Seconds between thunder & lightning, you
want to wait until the crashes & flashes sync. Can I teach
you to search out and test cracks in the sky? Your
hunger, I want to feed. Your recklessness, disarm. Child,
should you peek over the steep edges of cliffs to
know what's just beyond sight? Maybe. So we breathe
the wet, electric-charged ions, huddle tight, but when
the booms quake down to our sopping soles, the
gales swallow all choice. There's no way back. The world
breaks around us. We see what the storm takes
away, what it wastes. You're a witness, but your
voice—let's do it now. Yell. Curse the arbitrary air.

Broken Monster Sonnets

All the monsters are hungry at two in the morning.
Critters skitter in the attic. The bare, crooked
fingers of shrubs scratch at the siding. Outside
something wounded or alone screams in the trees.
Cold air hisses through the dry sashes,
phantom vapors—everything is losing heat,
shivering in the dark. The night doesn't know
winter is over. Just yesterday, fooled by the empty
sunshine, we turned the thermostat all the way down.
Still it's too soon for the tar streets to hold
any warmth. The brute sounds of cold night echo
in the thin air. My husband is asleep.
I've shut the glowing screens and pace barefoot
as time ticks sharp, starved, slow. A police car rolls up.

Next door lives a quiet, pained neighbor kid,
hair like straw, always smoking on the stoop
or walking someone else's dogs, everyday
reading his phone, head down. Tonight his mom
in her nightgown, shaking her head to the cops,
arms wide. No, they can't go in. Cherry lights strobe
through our windows, the drapes I hold askew
afire, then not. Some small kindness
from the police not to screech the sirens.
Monsters are everywhere, and mine checks the locks.
For years, I've seen that boy, his mom home late;
tonight her nightgown has ruffles at the knee.
I never meet his eye when he takes out the trash.
I never say *hey* when we pass on the street.

The Auction

A twisted antique flag rambles
                flexible and sinuous through the slats
        of old window shutters. Black paint flakes off the weathered wood.
            The faded blue, burnt red,
                  and flaxish white of the tired cloth
      so threadbare, the fibers
                      separate. Stars are missing.
(stars are always missing
      never where you think they should be)
The frayed flag won't again snap whip shots from a pole
           so gathers itself & weaves through misaligned louvers,
                drapes & climbs
                      the crooked wood like a vine.
Let's be honest. It looks like a student craft project.
          Upcycled attic scraps.
      Someone says it's a crime. Someone says it's stunning.
                    It picks a person to take it home.

I Dream What My Mother Means to Say

Here are the papers, important, ordered,
wrapped in rubber bands according to year
and account, and all the bills, by outstanding
and paid, but don't let that roofer fool you,
that sonovabitch, god forgive me, I paid him in full.

And here, the canceled checks for donations
I made every month to the church and the precious
Society of the Sacred Heart, for their beautiful
mass cards that I keep in shoeboxes if you need one
for a funeral now that everyone we know is dying.

And the jewelry, remember, I've already
divvied among you—my sweet girls and the boys' wives—
no difference, even that one who left. I'll never forgive her.
And whatever gold I didn't give away, I wear everyday
on a chain around my chicken-skin neck

because the rings slip from spindly fingers
I don't recognize. And the heavy anniversary pendant
bruises my breastbone like all these years.
Remember, it's under my blouse in case
an ambulance takes me alone and unconscious.

You can't trust anyone. And Dad's medicines are here,
even the old bottles with faded labels. Maybe they're
still good? He was always sick with something,
and if anyone needed a doctor, it was me,
but did I complain? And the tax bills are here,

and the annuity account, in my name alone. Remember
how he fell for Atlantic City? Those crooks. And the deed
to the house, which I've already signed over to your sister
because the rest of you had your chances at love
and you blew it or not, but she's still single,

and do not tell me again it's her choice and she's happy.
She gets the house. Don't argue with me now. I'm tired.
Everything aches since we lost your brother, my first,
the best of us, mine alone for a year. How could he drown?
He was so strong. I'll never understand.

What my mother really said, pausing at the foot of her bed
out of breath: *Look in this drawer when I'm dead.*

Flooded Odette's

The old river house,
refuge for bats and starlings,
keeper of cat piss, goose shit,
desiccated muskrat hide,
between the canal and the Delaware,
trading post, mule keep, tavern,
coal barge stopover,
river crew exchange,
gambling joint, dance hall,
cabaret, waterfront restaurant,
ruined heap and eyesore.
The fraying roof moldering at the rafters,
yellow caution tape around rotted floor boards,
crooked plywood nailed over glassless gaps,
an upended toilet behind a splintered cedar fence,
weather-smashed ribs of walls
watermarked six feet high,
carpet of dried mud,
punished stone footings
mortar pocked and shattering,
the blue-chalked X marking the spot
where the newscaster drowned,
gold-tipped arborvitae reaching for sky.
What to preserve, whose history,
whose stones?
Dusty wine glasses rest on the bar.
Yellowed postcards with that red ford out front
hang on bulletin boards all over town.
Egan's parties. Odette herself.
The roar of the river.
This holder of absence.

Twenty

after Patrick Modiano

Twenty again. That's where I'd go. Not to reinhabit a girl's taut skin
or ripe juiciness. Not to get strong eyesight back. Not even to be poised
to receive the great gifts on the way: my children or the love of a good,
good man. I want not the wisdom I've earned these decades since,

but the wide-eyed self-centeredness of twenty. I want to feel again
that it's no big deal to misplace my dead Grandmother's bundle of letters
from a brother in Italy, the ribbon-tied packet I think I left in my
professor's mailbox to translate. I don't know. I was going out with the gang.

That brother's name and village were written down nowhere else
but on those thin, folded and refolded sheets. Yet instead of scouring
the faculty office, 20-year-old me felt there'd be world enough
and time to find them, thought it infinitely more important to write little

poems of wonderment that summer while watching
a hummingbird through the window gather spider webs for a nest.
Hummingbirds have been plucking webs for millennia,
and no one on earth knows my grandmother's maiden name.

This is not my only sorrow. I don't want to understand it takes just
two generations to erase a history. At twenty you don't know
all you'll forget to tell. At twenty it's this moment, this moment.
You think nothingness is nothing. The world begins with you.

A Rural Metal Mailbox

In the oncoming headlights through the dusk,
a mailbox post looks like a deer. Vision
failing, plagued by floaters, who could
discern the post and rushing lights from darting legs,
hinds and hooves? At 40 miles per hour,

what you think you see is as real as fur and flesh.
You jerk the wheel, brake hard, the back end
skids out just short of the ditch. Pulsing
fear rises in the widening dark, churning
water. All this, and there is no deer.

The deaths I've known are like that,
some jittery thing not jumping out after you.
A familiar dock gone crooked in the ice,
a childlike trust of double yellow centerlines,
the weight of jagged air in brittle lungs.

You right the wheel and drive to a reading
where everyone shares at least one suicide poem.
It's not a theme. Though it is. Too many in the room
too ready, too hobbled, eyes askance
at what we see, shadows darting towards us.

Vreeland Avenue

Summer's end and nothing moved in that heat
except Uncle Tucky next door who was not
allowed in our yard. Just home from Saigon,
each day he fed trash to ashcan fires.

Mother yelled from the window: *Move away
from that fence. Go play dolls with your sister.*
He slouched on the stoop and tossed kindling bits
to the flames. I leaned so hard watching him

the chain link dented and cross-hatched my face.
I pressed my torso to the metal. Low smoke
burned my eyes. The cicadas' crescendo
rose in the trees. He was lost in the haze.

Yet the slap fixed him to me fifty years on.
Stop crying. Just leave that poor boy alone.

How to Eat Raw Herring

First, move to Rotterdam and marvel
at the patient art and grace of people
who rebuilt a city bombed to rubble
long before you were born. Walk along
the calm waters of the Maas with your young
daughters, your mother visiting
from New Jersey, and the Dutch crowds
waiting for the opening of de Erasmusbrug,
the Swan Bridge. Ignore your mom
who tsks and chucks her chin at the sculpted
taut cables and the asymmetrical
pure white (white!) single pylon, allongée,
ballet thin, reaching into the dusky sky.
When she says, *the Tappan Zee at home,
now there's a bridge,* skip ahead
on the embankment holding hands
with the girls. After the fireworks,
find the street vendor with the shortest line.
Buy the kids cones of frites and mayonnaise
but to your mother present with a smirk
a thin paper plate with two raw herrings.
Watch carefully as she balances the dish
in one hand, then swipes a fat finger-sized fish
through a mound of chopped onions.
When she tilts her head back and dangles
a whole herring by the tail over her open mouth
and winks (winks!), resist the urge
to tell your girls, who are fake gagging,
some smartish thing about grace.
You know nothing. Be a good Rotterdamer. Rebuild.

Gracie Clara Angie Rose

Often as a kid I stayed at my grandma's
rent controlled apartment in Hoboken near the hospital
where she in time would die. To help with chores?
To ease my mother's burden home with six other kids?
I always went gladly. Time alone was a gift.

My bachelor uncle came in surly after work
from the refrigeration warehouse. Silent and tall,
unaccustomed to children. Or movement, it seemed.
Or language. I didn't budge from the velvet sofa
until he took a dinner tray to his room and shut the door.

I was a challenging kid. Like Uncle was a bachelor.
Enduring adjectives back then colored all our stories.
Those sleepovers, no other kids near, Grandma's klatch
scootched a chair for me in the kitchen for their double-deck,
hours-long Continental Rummy games.

Gracie, Clara, Angie, Rose. Gossiped above my head,
fed me cards to make my melds. Their modifiers alive:
white-haired, thick-skinned, loud, St. Francis church women,
squeezed shoulder-tight at the speckled formica table,
sipping brown liquor from porcelain cups.

Those days. Shuffled stories. Tricks of time replayed.
I ache always at the sight of cobblestone streets
and brownstone stoops, run dreaming from the rusted
mouth of the terrifying garbage chute, crave
rectory leftovers wrapped in brown, stained paper.

And peering through these windows, there's the bus stop
on the corner, haunted, forbidden, where my mythical
grandfather sits eternally on the bus, taken
by an aneurysm; his cousin the driver, calling
Johnny, hey Johnny, are you sleeping or drunk?

Long gone, those ladies playing cards. That bachelor
uncle, dead now decades, forever grabbing
his hat from the rack, the heavy door slamming
behind him. Gracie, Clara, Angie, Rose,
in a warm room, always sniffing in their laughs.

My Missile Crisis, 1962

A flatbed truck slowly makes its way toward me
on the narrow stretch of York Road just past
the yogurt place and the Down Dog Studio.

It's a parade of sirens with an escort van, police car
and red flashers above a bright Wide Load warning.
For a minute I can't believe what I'm seeing—

a prone missile, rusted, muddy gray with a black band
round the nose cone, finless, longer than two truck lengths,
the width of the body tube encroaching over the double

yellow lines, pushing our northward traffic onto the shoulder.
It's a new world, I think, when missiles
can travel local roads to the Bucks recycling center.

And in that instant before I realize it's an old corn silo
and the world hasn't changed, I see my mother, barefoot,
pacing, wide-eyed in front of the TV, my younger

brother on her hip, her heels cracked and white—
country girl feet on a Hoboken kid
which to me even then just didn't seem right.

She runs her hand through her dark, bobbed hair
and when she notices me inspecting the face
the first time I see a person, not a mom,

she pays me back by laughing like someone I don't know.
*Is my hair a mess sweetie? It's all salt and pepper
until my next Miss Clairol shampoo.*

She turns to the screen, wiggles a pacifier
near my brother's lips. I suck the tips of my own brunette
braids, wishing for chocolate and tasting sweat.

Winter Dinner

When evening comes,
my mother reminds me again
to fill my father's pill box.
The job is done,
just as my sister taught me.
though Mother doesn't trust
that my attention to this task
equals love, my breathy sighs
pocked with impatience.
Lamps lit in a path to the bathroom,
hats and shoes laid out,
gas knobs off, fridge closed tight.
These few hours of dusky
dinner and game shows
a glacial night before I leave.

I cannot bear this slow decline.
My sister is kind.
She's here every day.
Thirteen years younger,
she tames belligerent pit bulls
and dives with sharks,
keeps a house spare
and swept clean as a shrine.
She tucks warmth into dusty
numbing tasks like a tissue in a pocket.
Which I never carry.
Which my parents need.

Where does grace come from?
There's zero Jesus in these lives.
The view from our childhood rooms
separated only by years, same trees
through the glass, same streetlights.
Maybe I was looking right
when grace descended,

and she was laughing
looking left—busses, squirrels,
over-bundled children on their way.

Mark Has a Thing or Two to Say About Those Strollers & Moms

I pulled Ginger back as she strained against the leash.
She wanted to jump and play near the parking meter
with that toddler who was escaping their parade.
A meandering parade, by the way, that blocked
the entire sidewalk. We couldn't pass them by.
We couldn't not see them. And that kid of theirs?
Precarious on the curb? How did I
refrain from grabbing him away from the edge
while they hollered across Union Street to each other
in the dusk after dinner, maybe mac and cheese,
trying to tucker out those sweet babies before bedtime?
Jesus. Can't stay cooped up when it's this nice out.
You guys doing soccer? Where'd you find that backpack?
School this. Mask that. Picture me shouting across the road.
The booming bass of an unknown man bouncing
off the bricks? I'd move away from the windows, too,
stir my dinner pots in silence,
pull down the shades.

        The Union Street shops are closed.
        Apartments in walk-ups glow with families
        coming home. And Ginger, poor thing
        in obedient sit, shakes against desire. The want of it all.

III

And some will stay up late beside the fire
On winter nights, whittling torches, while
the other runs the shuttle through the loom
And comforts the long labor with singing…

Passages from Virgil's First Georgic
4: 14-17, translated by Robert Fitzgerald

Tomato Intuition

"God made me this way, and I don't dispute it. Amen."
Flannery O'Connor

The cherry tomatoes sprawl and bury every other plant. God,
they're tireless. The peppers, chard, eggplants, beets made

into involuntary supports, smothered. New hairy stems daze me
each day like Jack's magic stalk. So dizzying, their reach. This

garden, planned in neat rows, now a fecund tangle. The way
I've been taught to tie-back or prune branches is useless. And I

finally surrender the need for control. The vines don't
hold back. Flower and fruit overflow. Who could dispute

these sweet and acid gifts to the tongue? Such a luscious mess. It
is time to give thanks for the persistent, the genuine, amen.

We Lived Where, How

That acrid basement kitchen on rainy days smelled
like a wet stable, doubling as our landlady's laundry

and litter box room, the odorous damp thick
with musty spores and dander. We didn't care.

Hasbrouck Place. Our first apartment. You built
our meager furniture. That glorious bed, a bookcase,

a table. Each measured, cut, pieced together
then stained walnut brown. None of it second

nature to you. And me, so full of doubt.
You studied woodworking tips and plans

for a week—dovetail joints, mortise and tenon,
routers and jigsaws—from an oversized, hardcover

Reader's Digest guide we had to shelve sideways
in the bookcase designed for thin volumes of poetry.

In that damp kitchen, I placed a yellow enamel
colander on the counter and hung a matching gravy

dipper from a hook. The color a deliberate plea for sunshine.
The gravy dipper never used, finally demoted to the junk drawer.

We've carried them to Cemetery Lane, The Renaissance,
Myrtle Street, Mohican, Leeuweriklaan, Roppongi,

River Road. Decades later, what remains? What will be
remembered? Our daughters will one day empty the house,

the enamelware will go to the thrift shops with all my books.
The bed is long gone, but that loose legged table

and bookshelf leaning out of square should become
(can this be my testament?) the fuel in a fire pit, smoke

rising to the gods who cradled us. Oblations. A boy
taught himself to build things, a girl to give them blood.

Dressing Yourself

I watch my grandson
navigate his morning clothes,
these undies, those shorts,
this shirt, who cares what color,
challenging what his three-year-old
brain knows of spatial geometry
and how he fits into the world.

He chooses a long-sleeve dinosaur tee
this 90-degree day
lays it on the floor, studies it,
naked, toddler pot-bellied, head bent,
arms snaking through the air practicing
the moves he needs.
Arms go there,
somehow head through there.
Kid tai chi and focus.

Then it's all cat and mouse with this shirt
push and pull, trial and error error error
until he gets it
and flattens a toothy T Rex over his torso.
He walks out bare butt and skinny legs
pleased and proud and present,
airplane arms, and without words shows me:
Look look what I can do now.

Tulips in Midwinter

Thank god in the cold for supermarket
flowers. Such extravagance—I bought three
lush bunches of tulips, though I wanted
so many more to mass in glass vases

on every surface in the house, vivid
oblong buds atop triads of fleshy
leaves and upright green stems. I wanted heaps
of deep goblets spilling gladdening hues.

I think of our Texel trip with the girls.
Biking the flat lanes through the farms, quiet
roads bordered by fields and fields of tulips.
Everywhere we looked, full blossoming rows

of yellow, purple, orange, and red playing
on our retinas until all the shades
blurred in the air beneath that grey Dutch sky.
We stopped. The girls ran up a sandy path

and knelt to hide inside the glow, their heads
and shoulders peeking above the buds.
This winter ache. A sea of tulips surrounding
our shining girls, dazzling and giddy with color.

Seeds

At the picnic table covered in newsprint,
he is up to his elbows in stringy
pumpkin guts. Five years old. Five pumpkins.
That's fair. Negotiated down from twenty.
He's slick and slippery, examining the seeds
and sinew, a tiny scientist, licking the flat kernels,
furrowed brow, focused. His mother wields
a butcher knife like she knows how to attack
and defend. Stay out of her way.
He paws through fibrous strands for seeds
that glue to his face, the back of his hands,
the bench; narrates plans for an improbable
garden, his belief in beanstalks to sprout fully
formed pumpkins in a week. I fight the urge
to teach. His mom just says, *we'll see.*
It's a crucial trick playing out here.
I must have done it once. But now unaccustomed
to such pure faith, I want to remember, to dissect
all this later. The air is sweet with a touch
of something more. Two identical trees have yellowed.
One is fully dressed, holding tight against the chill;
the other already bare, its gold skirt of leaves
promised and gifted to the roots and earth.
No doubt, that's where he wants to dig.

The Human Sundial at Jacob's Well

At the nature center holding your hand, I explain
how our shadows will cast a line to show the time of day.
It's a giant clock made of stones and wood and sun and you.
You are quick to add: *and ants, and air, and leaves, and sticks.*

Yes. Everything that's here in the park is part of time. Always.
Flat limestone bricks in the path are carved with the months
that you singsong like a nonsense nursery rhyme.
Wood logs set on end are branded in burnt numerals

for the hours and set in a semicircle of pea gravel, irresistible
for a boy who prefers sandboxes to clocks. You are tolerant,
though hours tick more slowly for you than me—
all fractions of time so weighty in proportion to your scant years.

The numbers on the dial, out of order to what you're
learning. It takes long minutes to fight the rote imprinted
pathways until we can read the dial together, starting at 7,
going round the oval to the crown of 12, then 1, and on to 6.

The sun warms your shining hair, you dig the toe of your shoe
through the pebbles, and I wonder how we might save these slow
moments as we race through our days. Decades between us. I search
for the mystical everywhere, or is this just a sweet piece of time,

a gummy to chew while we're doing other things?
It's 11:30, your young shadow says, in Wimberley, Texas,
this Monday in February. Can we travel back sometime
to the feel of our hands, to our voices under this slanting winter sun?

It's relative, I know. Whichever longitude or latitude,
whatever direction of the analemmatic sundial,
or the hours and months we balance on. Can this be a day
we come back to? It all depends on where we stand.

Still, I Smudged the House with Sage

The neighbors' virile hedgerow of maple
and white pine litters our driveway, clogs
the gutters. The neighbors fret. We rake and clear.
No worries. Autumn work in chill air is a balm.

They send their lawn guy over to castrate
the skinny bamboo phalluses that sneak
under the fence in every season. I suggest
hiring a goat. Adopting a panda.

They're 80. They settled on this well-worn block
30 years ago. We're green newcomers,
still learning the rasps and drafts of the house,
the rhythms of this genial street.

Then we discover the mirror in their trees,
bolted on a maple trunk, dark as an owl hole,
pointed toward our yard. In the slanted winter light,
we see our brick house reflected back at us.

They forgot it was there, the neighbors said,
hung decades ago to deflect the bad juju
of the home's ghosts, its troubles and savage
tirades. Wasn't that dog shit thrown over the gate?

Who called the cops, complained about fences,
parking, snow piles? Anonymous postcards
threatened lawsuits, called cordiality
conspiracy. Mute anger hung like fog.

It wasn't a feud, they said. Everyone
struggles and stress is alive. They believe
a skulking baseness roots in gray, hard pain.
They didn't want it growing in their yard.

Now we get it. The cheery waves. The large hellos.
It's not us. Just a deep exhale. And we don't mind.
Our windows are lit and sometimes clean.
The porch is big. The tomatoes ripe.

Lemon Tree Haiku

A thin, thorned sapling,
a green gift for Father's Day,
abundant in buds.

Star-pointed flowers,
fragrant, waxy, wanton throats,
profuse, thick blossoms.

The potted plant blooms,
self pollinates without bees,
lush near the window.

Such heady flowers,
deep aromatic bounty
from the stick-thin form.

Grateful, uncertain,
we water, keep the shades high,
wipe mites from the leaves.

A December snow
but inside the house, lemons
yellow and ripen.

January ice.
Curled citrus peels in the drinks.
The sun in our mouths.

A Black Stone

water worn with pleasing heft,
smooth, almost heart-shaped but lopsided,
the misshapen valentine we found
on that rocky Cape Breton coast, an oddity
so appealing that even Eros lost
in thought would have rolled it rhythmically
in his palm for long minutes before he
dropped it back into the sea. One lobe, distinctly
larger, and we joked half afraid on that misty
beach just three days after our wedding,
our bare feet raw in the surf, would this rock
be the mineral totem of our life?
Crooked, petrified, solitary.
Not us, we vowed. I snuck it home. And now
decades later, forgotten then found
again and again in the velvet-lined jewelry box
inherited from my mother, it's still solid, silky,
metamorphic, asymmetrical,
one lobe more hulky, forever beating
harder for the weaker side. The smaller
ventricle, sometimes me, sometimes you.

Tokyo Underground Prayer

On the Hibiya line, I watch my daughter laugh
with two friends: fourteen, long-haired, short-skirted,
their American legs in the aisles.
They snort and bend and poke each other into fits,
oblivious of other riders. Their
perfect faces crease with joy. And the way
their eyes glint, are those tears? I try to recall
a time when laughing was the only thing that hurt.

The train rocks and screams, the passengers
lurch silently, they clench and clutch.
All eyes behold the girls: swaying and floating,
their voices rise like balloons, like clouds, like hallelujahs.
Women on the train squint sidelong at them,
unsure what reserve of poise they need to step over
or ignore that tangle of candy toenails,
and flip flops, and legs, legs, legs.

Sit up straight and shush, I want to warn.
Close your knees. But I know just what they'd say.
Those pert new chests straining their thin tee-shirts
seem a tacit rebuke. I roll my shoulder-
blades back, hoping mindful posture will correct
what a good bra and calcium pills can't.
A gray-haired man in a suit sidles near.
He eyes these lives bubbling up before him,

just out of reach. His gaze swims on their bare skin.
I tense and my hard look says: Don't you dare.
The gully-lined scowl and hooded eyelids
of my weathered face should stop him dead.
Yet he moves nearer, cocks his head, and grabs
the pole behind their seats. He's close enough
to touch. He plants his feet and balances,
and I'm up, ready to charge, heart pounding.

But he rests. Clasps his hands behind his back,
in reverie, reverse supplication,
and poised, closes his eyes and sniffs the air
over their heads as if pausing in a garden
to remember some sweeter time. The girls
laugh, unaware. I ease back, raise my head,
and catch a whiff of a wafting honeyed scent.
I inhale a hint of holy incense. Then I let go.

Hotaru Ika : Firefly Squid

On the cliffs we peer down to the water.
A festival careens in the streets
behind us. Flags flap. Masked dancers
swirl silk ribbons. The drums pound a beat
I feel in my bones. Our breath quickens.
The smooth waves of Toyama Bay
swell and roll. The surface of the sea glows.
The squid are rising, burning for mates.
Gleaming lights alive in the crests glint
and fade, and then there, a few feet away,
again and again. The moon, low in a corner
of sky, is a sly wink at the slow pulse in the sea.

Your rugged face, lined. Gray curls touch your ear.
You strain forward through the crowd to watch
the shifting blue lights and reach for my wrist
without turning around. A current hums.
The parade moves on, and hypnotized
by the slow phosphorescence in the swells,
we hush with the locals. A young suited man
waits his turn, wipes the damp beads from his smooth
upper lip. He takes his place for a view
over the rocks and bows deeply,
long seconds to honor the water, the fish
that keep coming back, the light, this life.

The Masterpiece in Our Bedroom

San Girolamo, Caravaggio, 1605

In a dark room, San Girolamo writes
with a quill pen. He's partially draped
in a rich, red cloth, maybe a cloak, maybe
the covers from his bed as if he rushed
naked to the table straight from a dream
fevered with ideas. A thick book rests
on his lap. A thin halo's edge barely
visible above his balding pate hints
at hallowedness. For all the years I've dusted
this framed postcard on our bedroom dresser,
that little light remained hidden. The blessedness
I always see, what gets me every time—
the firm arm of a man reaching for—what?
a word? some truth? Muscled, alive, tendoned.
Only the holy of a bare-shouldered body.

Here's the tableau: the ancient saint stretches
without looking toward an inkwell in the shadows—
books, cloth, oaken table, and a blank-faced
memento mori. The man reads. The skull stares.
That hollow head a warning this world is fleeting,
the dark afterlife eternal. But, oh, Master, what
is your game? The skull is half hidden, a dull
paperweight, unheeded. Your model, bright,
vital, glowing with thought.

     I conjure you whispering, a voice escaping
time from that museum postcard on the bureau
while my love and I loll in bed—
Listen, before it's too late. Allow yourselves scarlet
bedclothes, and strong bodies in a glowing room,
and work you want to dive into, and books,
books are good, piles of them to retreat to,
partly naked, after rolling around
half the night with your love, alive, hungry
eating up this life and one another while you can.

My Daughter's Snakes

What makes us, at the same time, in different states
text each other photos of the shed skins
inside out of creatures scrubbing themselves new?

Focused, unfiltered on our screens, tight shots
of snake skins—litter you picked up thinking
plastic trash near your hot, rattling house

pushing the stroller, searching for blue sky
and a bit of green to please the baby,
and mine spied in the thirsty garden

like nylons waving on a line
but peeled from the slate under the buddleia
while I deadheaded shriveled and spent blooms.

One is head to tail complete, twenty-four
inches inside out onion paper thin,
eye sockets mouth hinge distinct scales right down

to the pointed molted end. The other
twisted, ripped, a thick wrist of a serpent
muscled enough to swallow small helpless

things whole. What gramarye connects us like this?
A full belly, then not? thick gravity?
the pull of blood through the ether?

Jinx! you'd call out, then link our pinkies and wish.
We can't look away—the wild tales seem true.
I helped a tiny you gather bones and moss,

flattened toads, bird feathers, antlers, and pods
for a nature box you kept in the garage.
You carried a live garter snake to show and tell

in a five-gallon bucket on the bus.
Remember? Let's say I wore these old
leather gloves, gnarled into the shape of my hands,

to catch serpents, fashion charms, or clasp my fingers
like a net. We didn't hide. We didn't ask
permission. Those spells we cast? I think they worked.

Mary Jo LoBello Jerome, poet, editor, freelance writer, and teacher, is a Pennsylvania Poet Laureate from Bucks County. She edited *Fire Up the Poems*, with a committee of poets, an anthology of creative writing prompts for teachers (2021) and is currently a poetry co-editor of *Schuylkill Valley Journal*. Mary Jo's writing has been published widely. She has lived and taught in her native New Jersey, Rotterdam, and Tokyo and has settled in southeastern PA with her husband. Read more at maryjolobellojerome.com

www.ingramcontent.com/pod-product-compliance
Lightning Source LLC
Chambersburg PA
CBHW030226170426
43194CB00007BA/873